EVANSTON·PUBLIC
LIBRARY

Purchase of this library
material made possible
by a contribution
to the Fund for Excellence

_____

_____

_____

_____

American Habitats

Desert Animals

Connor Dayton

New York

Published in 2009 by The Rosen Publishing Group, Inc.
29 East 21st Street, New York, NY 10010

First Edition

Editor: Nicole Pristash
Book Design: Greg Tucker
Photo Researcher: Jessica Gerweck

Photo Credits: Cover © Patricio Robles Gil/Age Fotostock; back cover, pp. 7, 9, 13, 17 Shutterstock.com; p. 5 © Bryndon Smith/www.istockphoto.com; p. 11 © Juniors Bildarchiv/Age Fotostock; p.15 © Steven Love/ www.istockphoto.com; p. 19 © Superstock/Age Fotostock; p. 21 © Armin Maywald/Age Fotostock.

Library of Congress Cataloging-in-Publication Data

Dayton, Connor.
    Desert animals / Connor Dayton. — 1st ed.
        p. cm. — (American habitats)
    Includes index.
    ISBN 978-1-4358-2766-0 (library binding) — ISBN 978-1-4358-3195-7 (pbk.)
ISBN 978-1-4358-3201-5 (6-pack)
    1. Desert animals—Juvenile literature. I. Title.
    QL116.D39 2009
    591.754—dc22
                                        2008036660

Manufactured in the United States of America

Contents

America's Desert Animals

A desert is a **habitat** that can be found in the southwestern United States. A desert's **climate** is generally hot during the day, cool at night, and very dry. In fact, some deserts get only a few inches (cm) of rainfall each year.

Despite the weather, America's deserts are full of life. You can find plenty of **reptiles**, **mammals**, **arachnids**, and birds living together in this habitat. This book will teach you about some of these animals. You will learn what they eat and how they live in such an interesting climate.

This is an eastern collared lizard. This colorful lizard is very common in the deserts of the United States.

The Dry Life

All living things need water to stay living, and water is very important to have in dry deserts. Desert plants have **adapted** to the dry, hot desert by making the most out of any water that comes their way. Cacti can store dew and rainfall that they gather. Other plants have **roots** that draw water from deep under ground.

Desert animals have adapted to the hot climate, too. Desert animals get a lot of their water from the plants and animals that they eat. Many of these animals can be found living in the deserts of America.

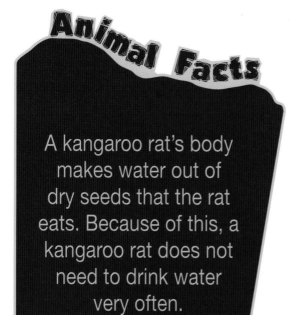

Animal Facts

A kangaroo rat's body makes water out of dry seeds that the rat eats. Because of this, a kangaroo rat does not need to drink water very often.

This picture shows prickly pear cacti (front) and tall saguaro cacti (back). These cacti store water so that they can live in the dry desert.

Where Are the Deserts?

There are several deserts found in America. The Great Basin Desert covers Nevada and parts of California, Oregon, Idaho, Wyoming, and Utah. The Sonoran Desert is in California and Arizona. The Mojave Desert, which is the driest and hottest desert in America, is in California, Nevada, and New Mexico. The Chihuahuan Desert lies in Arizona and New Mexico.

In these deserts, you can see how animals use their bodies to stay alive. For example, mule deer have large feet, which help them dig for water under the dry desert ground.

Animal Facts

A mule deer's ears are very large, and they stick out far from the deer's head. The ears let heat out of the deer's body. This allows the deer to feel cooler in the hot weather.

This mule deer is feeding on some grasses. Mule deer also eat leaves, branches, and vines that grow in the desert.

Cold Blood, Hot Habitat

Snakes and lizards are reptiles that live in America's deserts. A reptile is a cold-blooded animal. This means that a reptile's body **temperature** changes with the temperature around it. This is why you might see reptiles lying on hot rocks in the sun. The reptiles are warming themselves up.

One of these reptiles is the horned lizard. Horned lizards have horns on the tops of their heads. They may look scary, but horned lizards are harmless. However, they still try to keep themselves safe. Some horned lizards can spray blood from their eyes to scare off their enemies!

This is a desert horned lizard. A desert horned lizard's color is generally close to the color of the soil and sand around it, which helps the lizard hide.

Deadly Desert Snakes

Some of the reptiles that live in America's deserts are **venomous**. The sidewinder is a rattlesnake that lives in the Sonoran and Mojave deserts. This venomous snake eats lizards and small mammals. It gets its name from the S-shaped, sideways movements it makes over flat, sandy land.

The western diamondback is the biggest American rattlesnake. It can grow up to 7 feet (2 m) long. As do all rattlesnakes, the western diamondback uses its rattle to **warn** enemies. However, it is quick to use its deadly bite if it needs to.

Animal Facts

When a western diamondback gives its warning to its enemies, the diamondback curls up and raises its upper body. The diamondback can lift itself up 31 inches (79 cm) in the air!

The western diamondback, shown here, lives in the deserts of California, Arizona, and New Mexico. It is a symbol, or sign, of the American Southwest.

Hurried Hares

Mammals are also part of a desert habitat. The black-tailed jackrabbit is a mammal that can be found hopping around in open spaces or feeding on grasses and other desert plants.

Jackrabbits are not rabbits at all. In fact, jackrabbits are hares. A hare has longer ears and longer legs than a rabbit. Jackrabbits are fast, too. They can run up to 40 miles per hour (64 km/h) and jump up to 10 feet (3 m) in the air. Jackrabbits need to be quick because they are **prey** for many other desert animals, such as snakes, hawks, and coyotes.

Jackrabbits generally spend their days resting in the shade. If a jackrabbit gets scared, though, it will run for safety, as the one shown here is doing.

Coyotes

Coyotes are mammals that can be seen chasing and hunting their prey in the desert. A desert coyote will eat plants and bugs when there is little food, but a desert coyote likes to eat meat whenever meat can be found. Coyotes eat rats, rabbits, hares, and lizards.

A desert coyote's body has adapted to living in the hot desert habitat. Desert coyotes are smaller than other coyotes. These coyotes have thin fur that helps them stay cool in the hot weather. Their fur is also light colored, which helps them mix in with the desert's light colors.

Desert coyotes have strong senses. They can hear, smell, and see very well. Their senses help them find food and know where other coyotes are.

In America's deserts, you may spot an arachnid crawling on the ground. The desert tarantula lives in the Sonoran, Mojave, and Chihuahuan deserts. You will not miss the desert tarantula because it is about 5 inches (13 cm) long. It can also measure up to 11 inches (28 cm) from leg to leg across its body!

Another arachnid, the giant desert hairy scorpion, is the largest scorpion in America. It can grow to be up to 6 inches (15 cm) long. It has eight legs, two claws, and a venomous **stinger** at the end of its tail.

Animal Facts

The desert tarantula and the giant desert hairy scorpion may look scary, but their stings and bites are not deadly to people. Some people even keep these arachnids as pets!

Here you can see a giant desert hairy scorpion feeding on a bug. These scorpions also eat other arachnids and small lizards.

Desert Birds

Birds make their homes in desert cacti and bushes. The cactus wren builds its nest in strong cacti, such as the saguaro cactus. Then, the cactus wren flies down to the ground and uses its curved bill to flip over rocks to find bugs, fruits, and seeds to eat. The cactus wren gets most of the water it needs from these foods.

Turkey vultures are birds that live on rocky desert cliffs. Turkey vultures save **energy** by using hot, rising air to help them fly. Look up and you might see these birds searching for dead animals to eat!

Turkey vultures are America's largest birds of prey. Here they are shown resting on a cardón cactus.

Our Habitat

The animals living in America's deserts are used to having a lot of space. However, the desert habitat is becoming smaller because people are moving into it. When communities push into animals' habitats, the animals have nowhere to live.

The National Park Service, or NPS, controls parkland in all of America's deserts. The NPS makes sure that their parks are a habitat in which the desert's plants and animals can live. If you want to help, you can learn how on the Internet or at school. Then, you and your friends can help keep desert animals safe!

Glossary

adapted (uh-DAPT-ed) Changed to fit requirements.

arachnids (uh-RAK-nidz) Animals such as spiders, scorpions, and ticks.

climate (KLY-mit) The kind of weather a certain place has.

energy (EH-nur-jee) The power to work or to act.

habitat (HA-beh-tat) The kind of land where animals or plants naturally live.

mammals (MA-mulz) Warm-blooded animals that have a backbone, breathe air, and feed milk to their young.

prey (PRAY) An animal that is hunted by another animal for food.

reptiles (REP-tylz) Cold-blooded animals with thin, dry pieces of skin called scales.

roots (ROOTS) The parts of plants or trees that are underground.

stinger (STING-er) A sharp object on an animal's body that can hurt people and other animals.

temperature (TEM-pur-cher) How hot or cold something is.

venomous (VEH-nuh-mis) Having a bite that can cause pain or death.

warn (WORN) To tell someone or something that danger is coming.

Index

Web Sites

Due to the changing nature of Internet links, PowerKids Press has developed an online list of Web sites related to the subject of this book. This site is updated regularly. Please use this link to access the list:
www.powerkidslinks.com/amhab/desert/